SCHOLARSHIP FOR SOCIETY

Panel on Alternate Approaches
to Graduate Education

EDUCATIONAL TESTING SERVICE • PRINCETON, NEW JERSEY

CONTENTS

Note: Order forms for additional copies of *Scholarship for Society*
      can be found on page 61.

Panel on Alternate Approaches to Graduate Education

J. Boyd Page, *Chairman*
President
Council of Graduate Schools
in the United States

Daniel Alpert
Director
Center for Advanced Study
University of Illinois

Warren G. Bennis
President
University of Cincinnati

Albert H. Berrian
Associate Commissioner
for Higher Education
New York State Education Department

Edward E. Booher
President
Books and Education Services Group
McGraw-Hill, Inc.

Jean W. Campbell
Director
Center for Continuing
Education of Women
University of Michigan

Benjamin H. DeMott
Professor of English
Amherst College

May N. Diaz
Professor of Anthropology
and Director, Center for
Continuing Education of Women
University of California at Berkeley

Patricia Albjerg Graham
Professor of History
and Education
Barnard College and
Teachers College
Columbia University

Cyril O. Houle
Professor Education
University of Chicago

Robert F. Kruh
Dean of the Graduate School
Kansas State University

W. Edward Lear
Dean of the School
of Engineering
University of Alabama

Lincoln E. Moses
Dean of the Graduate Division
Stanford University

Rochus E. Vogt
Professor of Physics
California Institute of Technology

Albert N. Whiting
President
North Carolina Central University

I. Bruce Hamilton, *Executive Secretary*
Educational Testing Service

Sponsored by
Graduate Record Examinations Board
Council of Graduate Schools in the United States

PREFACE

In the fall of 1971, the Executive Committee of the Council of Graduate Schools and the Graduate Record Examinations Board approved the establishment of a Panel on Alternate Approaches to Graduate Education. A supporting staff was appointed at Educational Testing Service (ETS) and funds were provided by the Board. The Panel members were selected and invited to participate in the meetings that began in the winter of 1971-72. They were chosen not as representatives of the organizations with which they are affiliated but as individuals with widely varying backgrounds and expertise. All of them are dedicated to the highest standards of graduate education as well as committed to a search for solutions to some seemingly insoluble problems. The charge to the Panel was to examine graduate education with respect to what it is and what it could be, taking into consideration the need to respond to changing social circumstances. The hope was that the Panel members would interact to provide new insights and a better understanding of the complex process of graduate education, a hope that was fully realized.

It was made clear from the outset that the Panel was under no constraints other than time and the availability of support funds and that it could present a report expressing any point of view it so desired. *Scholarship for Society* is the result of the Panel's intensive study.

In all, five plenary sessions and several committee meetings have been held since early 1972. During that time, a number of staff papers were prepared. Several of their titles are listed at the back of the report and are available from the Executive Secretary at the Graduate Record Examinations office, Educational Testing Service, Princeton, New Jersey 08540.

Quite intentionally, the activities of the Panel were not broadly announced or publicized. Since we wished to pursue our work with a minimum of distraction, no ongoing reports were written, as is done by many commissions and councils. We were aware that at least two other national study groups were concerning themselves with the problems of graduate education, but the group felt that our contribution could best be made through the distribution of a final report to the sponsors and interested public rather than through other activities. During the course of our deliberations, the Panel conducted a mail survey of graduate schools and prepared a summary of the responses that can be obtained from the Panel office (see *Working Papers of the Panel*, page 59).

From the outset, the work of the Panel was coordinated with, but in-

PREFACE (continued)

dependent of, the activities of the Commission on Non-Traditional Study, chaired by Dr. Samuel B. Gould. Several of the Commission's studies and reports were of considerable interest and were used as references by the Panel.

During the early phases, the Panel ranged widely over the entire field of graduate education. Concern focused early on the structures and patterns of graduate education—accessibility, flexible instruction, restrictive requirements, and the effectiveness of graduate programs. As deliberations progressed, the Panel turned also to the spirit and meaning of graduate study, expressed ultimately in its recommendations. While the Panel recognized the need to maintain and strengthen major segments of graduate education, the recommendations are directed mainly toward alternate approaches of graduate work for the wider population of students now seeking entry into graduate schools and toward the creation of safeguards against excessive isolation in the graduate school environment. The Panel feels strongly that new elements do need to be added to graduate schools, that significant modifications need to be made, and that horizons of concern need to be expanded if graduate schools are to meet fully the emerging needs of society in the last quarter of the 20th century.

This report covers only a very small part of what was thought and what was said during the course of our deliberations. It has purposely been kept brief. It is not fully annotated in the formal sense but is an extended essay with accompanying recommendations. It should not be assumed that each Panel member agrees fully with every statement. But in the main, the thrust of the report accurately represents the intent of the group, and sums up the consensus eventually reached. We hope that it may serve to stimulate discussion and, ultimately, appropriate action. We have emphasized that there are new roles as well as a new clientele for graduate education, and we urge no less than a reevaluation of the basic objectives and organization of each graduate school and the disciplines essential to it. Out of such discussions may come a new sense of purpose and, where called for, an adjustment in priorities. We do not recommend revolution; we do urge increased sensitivity and considered response.

We offer this report not as an end but a beginning. If widespread discussion and thoughtful analysis result, we hope that the Council and the Board will do their share toward the implementation of appropriate recommendations and that others will feel impelled to join them.

I should like to express my appreciation to the Panel's sponsors, the Graduate Record Examinations Board, which provided financial support, and the Executive Committee of the Council of Graduate Schools, which made my time available for this effort. My sincere thanks go also to Educational Testing Service in Princeton, New Jersey, where staff support was provided. Panel activities were coordinated by Mr. I. Bruce Hamilton, Executive Secretary of the Panel. His contributions went far beyond provision of logistical support; they also included preparation of excellent background papers and supporting material as well as full participation in all of the affairs of the Panel. Key members of the administrative staff of ETS also participated in the discussions and provided invaluable counsel.

I owe special thanks to the individual Panel members who devoted so much time thinking about difficult issues and discussing various points of view in our extended meetings. Their patience with me and with one another and their obvious faith that there is indeed a way out of the difficulties now faced by graduate schools were most gratifying to observe. I wish particularly to thank Professor Benjamin DeMott who accepted additional responsibility for helping to distill the essence of our extensive discussions into *Scholarship for Society*.

As Chairman of the Panel on Alternate Approaches to Graduate Education, I am pleased to forward this report to the members of the Council of Graduate Schools, the Graduate Record Examinations Board, and to others concerned with graduate level education in the United States. We hope that the report will stimulate discussion and useful responses to the difficult issues that face the graduate community as new demands are made upon it.

J. Boyd Page, *Chairman*
Washington, D.C.
September 1973

I: ASSESSING THE PRESSURE FOR CHANGE

Is there an urgent need for change in American graduate schools? Two decades of increasing noise by the supporters of educational reform, the insistent rage for the new that seems to be part of our national character, and, finally, the decision of the Council of Graduate Schools and the Graduate Record Examinations (GRE) Board to appoint a Panel on Alternate Approaches to Graduate Education may make such a question seem tactless, evasive, or both. Should we not assume at this point that the central issues concerning change have to do with "how" rather than "whether"?

The Panel is aware of the widespread enthusiasm for innovation, indeed shares this enthusiasm. But it is also persuaded that the task of assessing the need for change is a complex undertaking. Our starting point has been the conviction that the sources of pressure for change are complicated, that the demands addressed to graduate schools are (on their face) contradictory, and that only when the contradictions have been examined and understood, does it become possible to think one's way toward sound policies for the future. It should be added that it has not been part of our fantasy to imagine resolving the contradictions; they and the attendant tensions seem to us stimulating and productive as well as confusing and troubling; we believe they will become more productive and less confusing when adequately understood.

Stock Responses to Change

A major obstacle to understanding the contradictions in graduate education is the persistence of stock responses—the tendency of opinion to freeze itself in polarities that reveal little except the differing preoccupations of the principals. Stock complaints about graduate schools state that they are inflexible about standards, unimaginative in developing optional styles of study, and remote from the realities of community life. Stock responses of graduate faculties describe these complaints as mere reflections of "traditional" American anti-intellectualism that display ignorance of the range and scope of activities carried on within existing graduate schools, and reflect the fashionable cults of relevance and permissivism. Both the complaints and the hostile responses blend truth and superstition, and communication depends on sorting out one from the other.

An indication of the intricacy of that task can be gained by considering the question of inflexible standards. It is well known that graduate schools are unofficial accrediting and certifying agencies, and that insofar as their standards serve as instruments of exclusion, they can be described as elitist. It is also well known that charges of elitism are usually made in a rhetoric of moral outrage. Why does the graduate school not admit everyone? With whom can it morally refuse to share its wealth? Does not the university care about human values, justice, decency, fair play? How can these minuscule Ph.D. topics, these dissertations on flea-sized subjects be justified? Shouldn't the graduate school exist for the health of society, rather than vice versa? When will the American graduate schools awaken to the needs of *people*?

We shall have something to say later in this report about admissions policy and the larger issue of the social responsibilities of institutions of higher learning. Clearly such responsibilities exist and can be better discharged than they have been in the recent past. One can go farther and concede that complaints against standards embody energies of democratization that have created levels of educational opportunity unmatched elsewhere, and that are indispensable to the country's future moral development. But no quantity of concessions will ever advance debate on these grounds beyond attitudinizing: The chief effect of political vilification of standards is to escalate a sense of righteousness on both sides and to obscure the matters that count.

The Problem of Standards and Functions

Among the most crucial of these matters—it lies outside the political orthodoxies of the educational right and left—is the relationship between standards and functions. Substantial differences of function exist among United States graduate schools and advanced degree programs, as has often been remarked. The major national, comprehensive university whose graduate programs and divisions are concerned largely with disciplinary and cross-disciplinary research may have standards that are pointless for assessing programs of graduate study at a state college serving regional needs in occupational training. Nevertheless, owing to habits of imitation and appetites for prestige, a single standard is sometimes invoked across the board. By confronting this complex situation, by relating patterns of assessment to function, by understanding that the preservation of standards demands their rational application, one can think about the theme of evaluation critically without indulging in sentimental egalitarianism. Such an evaluation carefully applied could conceivably earn full intellectual respect. But plainly, the first requirement is to transcend conventional ready-to-wear prejudices, both about elitism and about the decline of culture. And, precisely because "standards" has become a charged term, this is harder work than might be assumed.

Are There Enough Options?

A similar effort at transcendence is called for when assessing complaints about the lack of variety in graduate programs. Many graduate faculty members think this complaint displays ignorance, and once again their hostility is, in a measure, justified. Enthusiasts of structural innovation in graduate education are inclined to speak extravagantly, treating these institutions as a single great monolith, incapable of any substantive alteration. The litany of charges is by now familiar: "It's impossible to receive an advanced degree for talented original accomplishment in the arts" ... "impossible for a graduate student at any major university to define a field of interdisciplinary advanced study for himself and win acceptance for it, as a research project, from a graduate faculty" ... "impossible anywhere in the country to find a graduate school that actively encourages interdisciplinary work linking the arts and social sciences" ... "impossible to find a graduate school actively involved in and committed to external degree programs, to offcampus internship centers, or to any other open-plan advanced-education project." Without exception these statements are false. (The best current evidence on the point is found in the compilations on alternative learning programs published by John R. Valley, codirector of the Office of New Degree Programs, (1) cosponsored by the College Entrance Examination Board and Educational Testing Service. A mail survey conducted by the Panel revealed similar flexible programs within established graduate schools.) The resentment of graduate faculties who know the charges to be false, yet are obliged periodically to hear them out again, is natural.

Yet while zealots of the new are not invariably judicious in their account of the status quo, their exaggerations do not invalidate arguments for broader options. Rigidity is not the rule but multiple options are not the rule either. At Stanford University a graduate student can "invent" a new field of study and research for himself; then, provided that four faculty members join him and the entire proposal survives the scrutiny of a standing faculty committee, he can commit himself wholly to its exploration for his Ph.D. program. But the option is available at only a few institutions and is infrequently taken up where it exists. Discussion of pedagogical inflexibility, like discussion of standards, needs to be informed and particularized; usually it is neither, and here, too, the result is polarization.

Graduate Education and "Unreality"

Possibly the most harmful polarization occurs in contemporary exchanges about "unreality." Again the tenor of the complaints is familiar: Graduate programs are remote from problems as they exist in the real world; professors have too few connections with the world of affairs; when at length the graduate student is released into the world of jobs and men, he is befuddled, feels himself a stranger in an alien territory, cannot adapt his training to this living scene. Those who dismiss these complaints say that the American graduate school has proceeded farther than any other in linking advanced knowledge and research with the world beyond the gates. Consider the teaching methods of, say, a member of a graduate engineering faculty at a midwestern state university—or an agronomist at Nebraska or a metallurgist at Montana: Are these people seriously urged to adopt a more experiential or problem-oriented approach?

Furthermore, is it not a fact that much complaint about "irrelevance" arises, in the nonscientific fields, from students bothered by the ancient problem of adjusting their undergraduate and fragmented selves to graduate levels of concentration? Undergraduates are encouraged to a plethora of activities—performing on the playing fields and in the theater, experimenting with politics and sex, loafing, growing up—among which the two or three bouts a year of writing papers, plodding through reading lists, or prepping for "finals" frequently have the status only of interruptions. The step from here to the texture of life known by the graduate researcher is inevitably tricky and vexing. In some disciplines there is nothing to do but read all day, every day, most nights: read. In some disciplines the assumption is made that the graduate student's entire life shall be absorbed in study: Because there is an immense amount to learn . . . because to do one's own work well means knowing and profiting from what has been well done in the past . . . because why would one become a scholar in the first place except that he or she is moved by so profound a love of a subject that no hour spent at work, night or day, can seem drudgery?

The transition to such absorption is the more difficult, admittedly, because the rhythms of the scholar's day—the silent turning of pages or the examination of artifacts or the scrutiny of stills in the museum are as remote from the rhythms of a business or governmental world as they are from a day in the life of a fraternity sophomore. "Distracted from distraction by distraction"—the poet thus described, with a grimace, the quality of modern lives. But this quality is what most young men and women know, and to be set down in a context in which it is assumed that concentration and relative isolation will be the norms often creates unbearable strain.

But if discipline means anything, it means learning to savor what may initially have been unbearable. Therefore why listen to this fashionable new cant about offcampus components and the like? What does it add up to but an effort at legitimizing immaturity?

We need not itemize here the equally simplistic tones and attitudes of the passionate experientialists who hint that it is practicable to learn solid state physics in the streets, or propose that the single clue to the art of Tolstoy or Caravaggio is "exposure to raw life." Defining what can and cannot be expected from educational ventures in noncampus settings is complicated work, requiring detailed attention to differences among disciplines, and even, in some instances, dictating thoughtful reconceptions of the content of disciplines. The need is for a plan for offcampus enterprise sufficiently specific to permit substantive debate.

Defining the Conflicts

For this Panel, searching out issues buried beneath stereotypes, slogans, code words, and enmities has been a major part of assessing the need for change. We have tried to frame perspectives sharp enough to permit clear and explicit recommendations, while broad enough to permit a view of ambiguities in both questions and answers. In our opinion, beneath the rhetoric and contradictions, there are three major conflicts.

Democratization versus Preservation of Value

The first conflict is one that is formed by the tension between the thrust of democratization and the need to preserve value. The energies of democratization are pivotal matters of concern in planning for the future; the task is to harness these energies, while assuring the preservation of thought and perception. Every defect admitted, and every contribution to knowledge momentarily set aside, institutions of advanced study and research appear to be as strong and viable an embodiment of human capacity for delayed gratification, for unremitting labor toward a distant end, as our civilization has produced. Touched inevitably by materialism, by practical, local, and national self-interest, these cannot be confused with perfect places. Yet at their best they show us that people can have a purpose beyond getting and spending, namely that of intellectual self-development. They are more than assemblages of libraries and classrooms and laboratories; they *are* the ideal of cultivation both of self and of a field beyond the self as a decent human end. If the much-discussed ethos of democratic participation is to have any higher meaning than that of a protracted community sing, such ideals must be kept up. And, for the graduate school, this means ceaseless renewal of its own responsiveness to distinction, as well as sympathetic comprehension of the powerful American will to democratize.

Involvement and Mastery

The tension between the mastery of scholarship and the need for public involvement is another source of conflict. The words commitment and engagement occur more than once in the pages that follow, and this Panel is unanimous in its belief that the attitudes and behavior to which the terms point are essential to the vigor of teaching and of scholarship. We are also convinced that much more must be done to enable humanistic scholars and researchers in particular to perceive—and fully participate in—relationships between their knowledge and the problems facing a confused and fragmented society. But we have not underestimated the critical nature of the problem of balance. We concede that there is a need for the reconstruction or reconceiving of subject matter in certain disciplines in order that they may contribute knowledge to society from resources now relatively untapped. We also concede that scholars and researchers who are aware of the ways in which their fields figure in the daily lives of nonacademic adults are far more likely to perform with distinction as teachers; such awareness can also be an antidote to "value free" research heedless of the public interest.

Yet the effort at opening up the university and the disciplines must be governed by a sense of proportion, and by attentive concern for certain necessary and fruitful discontinuities between life inside and outside institutions of learning. If we are not in the business of training men and women for lives removed from social concern, neither are we intent primarily upon improving our own material lives or the on-the-job efficiency of the trial lawyers, city editors, yacht brokers, account executives, or new B.A.'s who enroll in our courses. Part of our value to students, young or in middle life or retirement, will disappear if we fail to maintain the conditions of a significant otherness, a measure of detachment from the common perspectives of ordinary life. We honor not only the principle of commitment but that of difference—difference of work style and life style—as well. The homogenization of occupation, the collapse of all differences of concern and purpose, is quite as harmful to the cause of teaching and learning, and to the quality of the general life, as is the iron separation of academic life in gated enclaves. And this will continue to be so as long as the pursuit of knowledge remains a minority taste.

Diversity and Order

The third conflict is that shaped by the tension between the values of diversity and order. Graduate education in the U.S. is presently conducted in an extremely wide range of settings. A moment ago the graduate student's life was evoked as—ideally—undistracted, unified, concentrated. To well over half the million-plus graduate students currently enrolled, this choice of adjectives can only seem ironic, for by choice or by need, they are part-time or intermittent students, discharging a variety of other responsibilities.

The graduate student may be a police sergeant studying two nights a week in a criminology seminar, a housewife-part-time high school English teacher commuting by car once a week from her suburb to an urban university; a young man whose uninterrupted cycle of study commenced at a private school and led on from Princeton to Yale; a young woman whose uninterrupted cycle of study commenced at public high school and led from a junior college to a state university; persons whose hope for a salary increment depends on the completion of another pair of credit hours; people whose lives are so variously harried—by anxiety about orals or ungraded blue books, or classes still to prepare—that they cannot themselves arrive at a coherent statement of their motivation.

Which is to reiterate once more that *the graduate school* embraces a variety of institutions and departments performing a variety of roles. We believe that the diversity of institutions is, potentially, the greatest source of strength that the system possesses. We also believe that at this moment diversity is a cause of chaos, and cannot cease to be until clear definitions of mission have been articulated and accepted by all parties. The desirable order will not be achieved by sealing off institutions from each other in a hierarchical structure. Neither will it be achieved by governmental commissions that gather together divergent institutions for purposes analogous to the reading of a will. Effective order depends instead on the development of close working relationships among graduate institutions themselves and among these institutions and their undergraduate and secondary school affiliates. Levels of understanding of role and function are needed to make it possible for each kind of institution to contribute to the work of the others unselfconsciously, uncondescendingly, and in the spirit of equals performing divergent honorable tasks.

A Reasoned Response

Attempts to respect the environment of hard issues, to weigh alternatives on a delicate balance, often draw criticism as "middle of the road," "unimpassioned," and the like. We have preferred to run the risk of such criticisms, rather than to sacrifice our conviction that accepting or resisting change is essentially meaningless if unaccompanied by a realistic survey of the surrounding terrain. We have also preferred not to operate on the assumption that the problems of education in America compose a seamless whole, in which distinctions between undergraduate and graduate education are illusory. The Panel has profited greatly from the explorations of new avenues conducted by the Commission on Non-Traditional Study (2) and others; but it continues to believe, partly because of the role of graduate schools as trainers of teachers, partly because of the ongoing role of graduate schools in the development of the disciplines (and cross-disciplines), that the undergraduate model cannot everywhere be accepted as a norm for graduate education.

Our hope is that the conclusions and recommendations in this report compose a reasoned response to what can be described, without exaggeration, as unprecedented needs and unprecedented opportunities. In working toward that end, much of our best guidance—keys to emergent values, evidence about the character of inner systemic strains—came to us by way of reflection on history. We turn now toward that guidance.

II: HISTORICAL PERSPECTIVES ON EXPANSION AND RETRENCHMENT

New realities flowing from declines in federal support and in employer demand for graduate-trained workers have induced an understandable but error-prone crisis psychology—in itself a more considerable source of confusion than any of the stock responses discussed previously, and demanding, for that reason, separate attention. An historical perspective can help dissipate a crisis psychology because it can restore to view long-term trends that vanished from sight at the "bust" moment in the sequence of boom and bust. Such a perspective can also disclose the relationship between the almost overnight loss of a sense of mission and some forms of "cultural lag" possibly unique to universities.

Interpreting the Current Mood of Depression

When this Panel was conceived, heavy tremors of concern about over-expansion had already passed through the university community. And at the present writing policies of cutback and retrenchment are in force in many of the country's graduate departments. Viewed in terms of existing job markets, these policies may make sense. The rate of production of doctors of philosophy between 1967 and 1972 was such that, had it continued, some 50,000 to 75,000 Ph.D.'s a year would have been entering the labor market by 1980, the majority of them without hope that the degree would guarantee either teaching or research employment. As it is, even with the cutbacks, no matchup has been achieved between the number of university positions and the number of jobseeking Ph.D.'s: On completion of their work for the doctorate, less than half the present graduate student population will find employment within academies, and many in the population who wanted positions in industry and elsewhere may find that these doors too are closed. (For graduates in the humanities and social sciences, to be sure, the absence of academic employment opportunities is a more critical problem than it is for graduates in the natural sciences and engineering.)

Like every period of retrenchment, the latest turn of the cycle has created a mood of depression. It can be agreed that the skills of the Ph.D. who finds work in business or in high school teaching should not be thought of as wasted, and, further, top-ranked graduates in all fields continue to find university employment if they desire it. Nevertheless, the human costs of recent miscalculations about job markets cannot be disputed. Those miscalculations have resulted not in mere number gaps, but in states of despair and anger within human beings; when fair account is taken of the feelings of the many well-trained but unlucky jobhunters who have been traveling the lobbies and halls at recent professional association meetings, cool talk of miscalculation seems heartless. The current psychological depression is, in other words, wholly understandable.

Yet it must be added that the opinions about the academic future that have formed under the influence of this depression are, on balance, untrustworthy. Among these opinions are some that now seem to be hardening into a new conventional wisdom: America has gone as far—or farther—with the extension of advanced education as it is practicable or desirable to go; boomtime euphoria—the force that spawned multitudes of state universities, scores of new community colleges a year, and fresh annual crops of private research firms on the fringe of major university centers—was out of touch with the true capacity of the nation to carry forward higher education on a mass scale, and perhaps with the true desires of the populace as well; endless expansion in higher education could be actually harmful to the national interest.

In the opinion of this Panel, such wisdom is wrongheaded. Nor are any vast resources of ingenuity or brilliance necessary to demonstrate that this is so. Higher education has continued to strengthen its place among the growth stocks in the economy. The demand for expertise varies widely, within fields, within narrow bands of time; within the culture as a whole, the course of that demand has been upward throughout the century, and both existing and predictable technological and social configurations suggest not a declining but an increasing need for specialized intelligence in the future. Meanwhile, the pool of citizens at every age who are capable and desirous of education at advanced levels continues *its* rapid expansion. The rate of increase in B.A.'s from year to year is slowing and may even decline in the 1980's, but higher enrollments in community colleges and other two-year institutions more than offset that trend. A plausible guess about the future is that the student population of many graduate schools will include substantial numbers of two-year college graduates whose subsequent work experience is offered and accepted as justifying equivalency admission; such students are less likely to be degree-seekers, and their educational aims will surely be different from those of "traditional" graduate students.

Nevertheless, the aims of non-traditional graduate students will be genuine, and graduate schools and society should attempt to gratify them. Many Panel members have repeatedly expressed doubt that the implications of the community college movement in this country are as yet accurately grasped. The meaning of the movement cannot be fathomed simply by remarking on society's surprising willingness to extend the right to 14 years of free public education to its citizenry, or by considering only the movement's "career education" aspects—specific training programs in nursing, computer programming, and the like. We also need to note that community college course offerings are by no means exclusively vocational; many provide the student with opportunities for speculative thought about the content of the moral life, the nature of the principles of natural order within the universe, the possibility of a religious faith, contemporary conceptions of culture, belief-systems, myth, the unconscious, and so on. The commitment to two years of college may have been thought of originally by many people as a vocation apprenticeship—a boost toward the "upward mobility" conveyor belt. But in countless actual institutions it has become a commitment to Dostoyevsky, Levi-Strauss, and the laws of nature as appropriate, even necessary, materials for the development of self—and, beyond this, for the development of a nation of individuals who are capable of reflection.

If Everyman is to profit from personal inquiry into such subjects as the ethics of crime and punishment, new arts of teaching will be necessary. But to return to more general consideration of the market, it cannot be assumed, merely because various polls and projections indicate that several million Americans are interested in taking a course of graduate study at some future date, that no limit can be set on the number of future consumers.(3) What matters most, though, is that there is a steady increase in the number of Americans who have been exposed to some significant intellectual labor and who can imagine what it is like to treat social and personal issues as well as technological challenges philosophically and analytically. And this increase continues the patterns of the past.

The great expansions in the history of American education—the founding of public elementary and secondary schools, the establishment of the land-grant universities, the funding of the GI Bill of Rights, and most recently, the enactment of a federal scholarship bill—have not been part of any articulated, orderly plan for the self-development of Americans. Often in the past, the system has seemed about to settle into stasis and enclosure. But the current of expansion has regularly renewed itself and has remained, historically, the dominant current. Those persuaded by recent setbacks that its reversal is imminent appear to us oblivious to the deepest American aspirations.

The point asks to be stated even more strongly when certain of the culture's emergent needs and longings are examined. Several motives currently gathering force seem bound to intensify popular interest in the life of learning—and in the university—provided the university can teach itself to be responsive to this interest. Though the limits of the present report permit no large-scale culturological survey, it may be observed, briefly, that two influences among younger people—the preoccupations with ecology and with personal self-development, spiritual and intellectual—obviously bear on the future appetite for advanced and recurrent study. The increased number of people who are critical of lives devoted to material accumulation is among the most striking events in the history of modern sensibility. Whether this consensus grows from respect for the environment or from awakened interest in the moral imagination, its effect as a stimulant to the pursuit of knowledge and the development of reflective power could well be immense.

"Could well be" but not "Must necessarily be": History does not underwrite prophecy. It does, however, as this survey should have made clear, provide a basis for criticism of the more mindless pessimisms of the present hour. The long-term trend of expansionism, the available research in the area of popular desire for further education, the developing spiritual aspirations among the young—all these attest that the current depression and wariness in the graduate sector could be excessive: a gloom-cloud obscuring major growing points.

The Problem of Cultural Lag

If one could be certain that a simple statement of the reasons for long-term optimism could clear the air, the problem of attitudes about the future would not need to concern us. But, as it happens, those problems cannot be so easily passed over. For they originate not alone in budget cuts but in fundamental failures of adjustment to the situational and functional changes that have occurred in the university over the last half-century.

Many educators have commented upon the extraordinary transformations, both of scale and in range of operations, undergone by the American university in the past decades. "In 1968," writes Harvey Brooks, "the percentage of the age cohort receiving Ph.D.'s in science and engineering and medical or dental degrees was higher than the percentage of the corresponding age cohort that received bachelor's degrees in 1920."(4) In 1968, the rate of increase for Ph.D.'s in the humanities and social sciences as compared with B.A.'s in these fields in 1920 was lower but still striking. And there have been many comments about the extraordinary transformations, both of scale and in range of operations, undergone by the American university.

What has not been made clear is that these changes in scale, by dramatically altering the relation between the university and society as a whole, have necessitated thoroughly different self-conceptions on the part of teachers from those that were appropriate a half-century ago. Perhaps an absence of change in self-conception more than anything else has created a vulnerability to crisis psychology and to the other insecurities and confusions of the present hour.

Faculty Psyche, circa 1920

Can the academic self-image prevailing two generations ago be recovered for purposes of comparison? Not, surely, with precision. The best we can provide ourselves is an informed guess or two. Guided by relevant historical information, and alert to exceptional situations (the development of the university of public concern, as in Wisconsin, and the growth in the south of the Black colleges), we can imagine a probable pattern.

A half-century ago the academic professional would not have been wrong to have understood himself to be a member of a tiny, marginal order. He could have believed, with justification, that society and government neither cared about his interests, nor felt impelled to share them, nor would have been other than bored or resentful if invited to share them. He had few reasons or none for regarding himself as a worldly man, and he understood that employment opportunities for persons holding the doctorate were limited. (A scientist might exercise choice between a post in a corporation or a government research laboratory, but an academic environment was more likely even for him; as for his fellows in the humanities and social sciences, no other place of work was imaginable.) As nearly as he could make out, there were but two respectable models of the professor as teacher: In the first, the professor was a research scholar offering instruction, in laboratory and seminar, to research scholars in embryo; in the second, the professor was a small-college humanist, offering a model of general cultivation to young men and women, often of comfortable circumstance, most of whom would end their days of study abruptly and permanently upon receipt of "the sheepskin." Finally, our Earlier Academic Man may well have had a private understanding with himself that, with a few exceptions over the years, his undergraduate students did not need a clarification of values or ways of coping with an overwhelmingly bewildering cultural prospect. For the most part they were visiting the institution of learning as a social obligation, questing for "manners" and "contacts" more than for ideas that might change their lives. At the graduate level guidance was likely to be directed as well to those already committed to professional training.

Now to contend that these beliefs survive in the university of the 1970's is not to assert that they are to be found, perfectly fossilized, in any single faculty member or administrator. As we have just said, it is commonplace among our kind that the academic profession is larger nowadays; that there are more journals to read; that state teachers colleges have somehow changed in nature; that government grants are pivotal to the life of some departments; that certain urban institutions have been organizing task forces to combat urban problems; that swarms of undergraduates go on to graduate school; that Ph.D.'s are required for many jobs in city, state, and federal governments, in think tanks and in testing services, in welfare and community agencies and in a dozen different varieties of consulting firms. These facts are "known," but in the opinion of the Panel this knowledge exists at too low a level of consciousness and has too little effect in shaping academic self-definitions.

Endorsing Yesterday: Outmoded Peer Ratings

That a consciousness of change has been slow is in no way puzzling, for while extraordinary changes have occurred, extraordinary steps have been taken, by accident, by intention, and also as a simple result of habit, to treat the changes as peripheral events. One example: An academic man or woman of the 1970's bent on securing objective assessment of his own and his immediate colleagues' labor, can turn to ratings published by the American Council on Education and discover that his department is evaluated as "Distinguished," "Superior," or "Good" (or ignored), and that the yardstick employed—quality of original contribution by individual department members to advanced knowledge within the discipline—is precisely the same as that which would have been acceptable in 1920.(5)

If the faculty member serves mainly in an interdisciplinary, urban, or environmental program, or in an institute for the development of new technologies, he will not find himself counted. If the faculty member serves in a traditional discipline, but in a significantly innovative department—for example, Michigan State's Department of English, which has conducted pioneering experiments in linking the training of literary scholars with that of elementary-level, ghetto-based teachers of remedial reading—*he* will not find himself counted. The models of university reality and accomplishment that *are* acknowledged are those whose shape was firm in 1920. And the places perceived as "Distinguished" are, more often than not, those whose forms and ambience—from the commons rooms and the gothic gates to the occasionally embarrassing pride in "highly selective admissions policies"—imitate those of institutions founded in the world of kings and mass illiteracy.

The foregoing remarks are not meant to deprecate prestigious older universities; the Panel does not believe in the eradication of difference among universities or between the university and society, or in a total commitment by graduate schools to relentlessly relevant, socially pointed programs and research, or in the abolition of pure intellectual distinction. But we do feel that the single standard rating system is one way in which contemporary academic professionals are inhibited from assigning the proper weight, in their own minds, to the vast changes of function that have been in process over the last few decades. And we are arguing that the practice of referring all contemporary educational enterprise to a single traditional norm weakens the sense of the importance of the great, ongoing national experiments in mass higher education, and in the use of the university as a resource for meeting social problems.

22

Further, we are arguing that the consequence is waste: Leaders who could contribute to the newer educational enterprises of the age, without sacrificing their power to advance their own disciplines, fail to make that contribution because they are unaware of how the divergent parts of "the system" might work together.

Three Professional Profiles

The subject becomes clearer when one approaches it in terms of illustrative persons. Professor E. L., a graduate faculty member at a major research-oriented university, lives in an urban area that also boasts both a community college and a branch of the state college system. His considerable reputation is built on a series of contributions coauthored with his graduate students, each paper in turn adding another block to his research design. (Few women are allowed on his team—they aren't, he thinks, "serious.") His chosen students usually move directly into the industries that support his discipline, but in recent years they have found challenging positions more difficult to secure. Professor E. L. is concerned but tends to dismiss this problem as part of the chance one takes upon entering graduate study.

Although he is widely known for his research, he has little contact with other members of the faculty outside his own specialty. He assumes the neighboring colleges do something of use but he has no real conception of why they exist except possibly to take care of the swarms of students his university rejects.

Arthur K., Professor L.'s former student, is the 28-year old chairman of his department at the community college just mentioned, and a dropout from the research university Ph.D. program. Arthur has taught himself to despise the university department for its "cavalier" disregard of the needs of students at "this level." These students can learn, Arthur fervently believes. He is convinced they have it within them to make the subtlest discriminations, to create a significant canon all their own.

Yet Arthur is often frustrated and acknowledges to himself that he needs help. On occasion his students respond beautifully to the insights of his discipline, but when asked to perform the verifying scholarship typically asked of students at the research university, they shrug it off, become sullen, and complain of irrelevant makework. He is not certain what the best approach to his discipline should be. He feels he cannot turn to his former professors for help: The language, the attitudes, the erratically participational enthusiasms and naivetés he has grown accustomed to are of a kind "those elitists" could not begin to comprehend and would doubtless dismiss as hopeless. Arthur has, therefore, made a complete break with the graduate faculty once well known to him and, to his cost and that of his students, is envenomed in defensive contempt.

23

One faculty member at the state college, Mrs. C. H., knows Arthur as well as Professor E. L.: Her husband is a colleague of E. L.'s at the university and she knew Arthur as a graduate student. She finds teaching at State a terrible burden: huge, impersonal classes with no readers or other help, and no time to do other than prepare for the next crushing class. Few of her students take to her discipline; most seem satisfied to learn only the rudiments. With thousands like herself, she yearns to teach bright students and cannot locate significant intellectual challenge in her present job. She views her students, many of whom transferred there from Arthur's college, with sympathetic dismay. Meanwhile, convinced that one can "publish one's way out of any place" despite the barriers she feels exist for a woman in higher education, she pushes herself hard at night and on weekends, rewriting (without great pleasure) her thesis for publication in journals whose readership is possibly smaller than that of her present classes. Although her husband understands her plight, she is not encouraged by him or his colleagues to any wider view of her situation than simply that it is "bad luck."

To describe these people as illustrative is in no sense to imply that they are typical, or to deny that a multitude of other academic postures exist— among them, many that are more in keeping with genuinely democratic aspiration. Yet if the profiles in question point at a common behavior in any number of educational institutions, they are a measure of a troubling contemporary dilemma.

Current Trends: From Dropouts to Minority Admissions

There are other consequences of the present low level of consciousness besides the waste of teaching resources. Not the least of these, in the Panel's view, is the continuing tendency to box problems separately, even though they are interdependent. And the large new realities of which they are merely symptoms remain obscure. The rate of dropout from Ph.D. programs, the inadequacies of the present degree structure, the need for new testing techniques that will reveal the kinds of teaching-learning situations best fitted to individual talents, flexible programs for women candidates, minority admissions—these problems cannot be solved, true enough, by sanctimonious statements of goals and ideals. Neither, though, can they be profitably addressed in isolation from each other, or from a perspective that ignores the relationship between these problems and the new concepts of university function and responsibility to which they owe their very existence. The Panel has separate recommendations to make (see Chapter IV) concerning each problem cited, but all of them are essentially interpenetrating and we are convinced that before any recommendation can be effective, there must be a recognition that certain academic self-images of a half-century ago are obstacles to new breakthroughs in American experiments in mass higher education.

Summary

In common with special forms of academic cultural lag, the cycle of boom and bust through which graduate education has recently passed has badly clouded perceptions of roles and responsibilities. Responding to a series of shocks—a period of militancy and protest, followed by funding cutbacks, followed by a squeeze in the job markets—some voices have maintained that graduate schools are overextended, that they have victimized an entire nation with their presumptions. Some teachers and administrators have, in consequence, slipped from a mood of depression into a species of academic pastoralism—dreams of a retreat from the center of national life. But examination of historical trends and research on the future market for advanced education, indicates that the vision of retreat can never be better than a fantasy. Graduate schools in particular possess at this moment central positions and obligations in addition to the original duties of advanced institutes (the preservation of traditional knowledge and the advancement of learned disciplines). Three requirements for meeting the obligations, new and old, are the following: 1) awareness among academic men and women of fundamental directions of American society; 2) readiness among faculties and administrations to criticize their own self-conceptions in light of historical shifts in the place of the learned professions in the general life; and 3) an appropriate philosophy of change, alert to human hope as well as to human needs.

III: A SOUND PHILOSOPHY OF CHANGE

As we have already implied, an adequate philosophy of change in graduate education should evolve from a knowledge of what must not be lost: the inviolable cultural capital represented by existing forms of graduate training. But such a philosophy calls for much more than respect for tradition. It is essential to be alert to the character of contemporary pedagogical resources (theoretical advances in understanding of the processes of learning, technological advances with a bearing on the diffusion of knowledge). It is also essential to be familiar with the present obstacles to the delivery of knowledge—structures and forces that lessen the social effectiveness of specialized knowledge, and educational emphases within graduate institutions that might increase this effectiveness. Finally a satisfactory philosophy of change must embody and articulate humane ethico-political goals, over-arching yet realistic.

Participation and Individualization

Inevitably some of these specifications are easier to meet than others. In common with most members of the learned professions, the members of this Panel are in no doubt whatever about some essentials in advanced education and research—objective intellectual standards, criticism by peer group, and a proportioned sense of the claims of the past and future as distinguished from those of the present. The Panel is equally clear about the broad directions of change suggested by contemporary theoretical and technological advances. In some disciplines these directions were evident long ago: Collaborative scientific research by student and teacher in the laboratory is generations old. But modern educational theory has extended the lab science model to all disciplines. A student is no longer considered an empty container to be filled, and teaching-learning situations are considered moments of reciprocity, occasions in which professor and graduate engage jointly in the pursuit of knowledge. The hardware and software of modern education—cassettes, tapes, films, xerography, computer-assisted instruction, cable television, paperback publishing, flexible study modules—have made programs of study that are directed by students themselves both off and on campus not only possible but increasingly attractive to the mobile, independent students who

27

are seeking graduate study today. Participation and individualization, in short, are the themes that rise up vividly on present theoretical horizons. And in the Panel's proposals for change, we have tried to respond to these themes.

Barriers to Social Effectiveness

Assessing the forces that currently reduce the social effectiveness of advanced knowledge is a rather more difficult task than defining nonexpendables or locating the weightiest theoretical trends of the hour. Yet while conclusions came more slowly, the Panel did at length reach a consensus. Central to it are two beliefs: The first is that the present organization of intellect and the allocation of research resources and funds are major obstacles to the successful consideration of social needs by specialized intelligence; the second is that social effectiveness varies directly with the nature of the models of career orientation directly or indirectly endorsed by graduate institutions. Stated negatively, this means that graduate institutions do not press hard enough to extend the standards and methodologies of advanced research into public areas. Stated positively, it means that graduate faculty who are immersed in problem areas influence by example. Many of their students emulate them and strengthen their own commitment to careers involved in problem areas.

As is evident, detailed suggestions about how to foster the growth of socially productive intellectual models are necessary if the point just made is to register as something better than a truism. But we must add that in this area changes of attitude are no less essential than modifications of structure or allocations of resource. A sane philosophy of change must ask what areas researchers should be encouraged to enter, and it must also face the subtler matter of the spirit in which *all* graduate study, regardless of area, should be conducted.

What are some possible changes? This Panel favors drawing greater numbers of students in the natural sciences away from minor basic research careers and toward what one Panel member has described as "occupations related to planning for the servicing of social needs." Such a goal is not hostile to basic research; we are merely expressing agreement with those who concluded, before us, that the kinds of perspective, the habits of relative objectivity characteristic of advanced research need to be brought closer to serving social needs. Current examples include graduate departments and divisions that consider faulty delivery systems for medical care or low productivity in elementary education to be perfectly suitable subjects for large-scale research. Such studies begin to expand the uses of advanced knowledge. And, as we said, several of the Panel's recommendations aim at increasing the commitment of self-selected graduate faculties to such inquiry.

Process versus Product

Increased commitments by faculties and students to socially oriented research can help close the gap between knowledge and society; so too can efforts by leaders in disciplines other than the natural sciences to define the public dimensions of their research. But we return again to the issue of style: The matter of what is studied is of no more consequence than the way in which the study is conducted, or the way in which the student conceives the relation between himself, as student, and society as a whole. In our view, a system of tacit understandings about advanced education has grown up over the decades that has tended to imprison the professionally trained researcher within the local culture of his discipline. The burden of these understandings can be expressed as follows: The product is all, the process is nothing. Guided by elders, and by the realities of careerism, graduate students in many disciplines place themselves psychologically on a line of progress toward The Degree: x months to the completion of the residence requirement and course work, x months to the passing of orals, x months to the acceptance of the dissertation subject, x months to the completion of the research, x months to "writing it up." There are, to be sure, exceptions: disciplines and institutions in which a confident feeling of "in-touchness" is the norm for students. But for far too many students the period of advanced study exists as a mode of suspension, a block of time somehow cut out from life, totally set apart.

We have spoken earlier in defense of an experience of absorption in study, and have granted the desirability of maintaining a reasonable distance between the university and the public world, and we do not retreat from either position. But we seriously doubt that much purpose is served by narrowing opportunities for the graduate student to the graduate institution and its departments. We believe that the values and satisfactions of participation in a life beyond that of personal self-development can and must be experienced during the training of the graduate researcher; these satisfactions should be assumed to belong to the process of advanced education in every field, not alone in those scientific and engineering fields in which student-faculty participation on lively research teams is common. Years of study must not be years of isolation; rather they should be a time of active engagement with peers in undertakings that have immediate and visible consequences for the quality of the surrounding life; the notion of study as an interminable staging area, a postponement of "real life," is unacceptable. Reforms in governance systems can enable graduate students to play roles in shaping institutional policy and can enable them to serve in problem-solving team efforts within departmental and cross-departmental groups. Improved communications within existing departmental structures can enable students to participate in decision-making about broad research commitments. And by their exploration of certain subject matter areas they can introduce problem-solving components into studies that were previously enclosed in a grid of coursework. These changes can foster a new literacy in dealing with complex issues and new participational skills in solving the problems raised by these issues.

Of course the mastery of many subjects cannot be achieved through team efforts. To transform the editing of the Roman poet Persius into a problem-solving venture with immediate consequences for the general society is, at first glance, impracticable, and perhaps at last glance as well. Extended solitary labor will remain, in certain disciplines, the *sine qua non* of achievement. Still, we are convinced that much graduate education is needlessly overcommitted to structures and attitudinal "fixes" that intensify feelings of disengagement, of remoteness from community, and of chilling disbelief in the social uses of knowledge and imagination. The Ph.D. who is heedless of social reality and of the obligations and opportunities of specialized intelligence has, in a sense, been taught his heedlessness by the conventions of the system itself. A philosophy of change capable of serving as a support and guide to rational day-to-day policymaking must be conscious of the alienating effects of these conventions, and must work toward their abolition.

An Ethico-Political Framework

To recognize the need for over-arching goals is to be tempted toward moral exhortation; the Panel has sought to resist this temptation. It has not been possible, however, for us to arrive at a series of coherent recommendations for the future without glancing more than casually at concepts of ultimate purpose, and, at the risk of repeating sentiments which to some must seem obvious and to others controversial, we think it sensible to comment briefly about our understanding of social goals and our conception of ways in which advanced education can serve them.

The heart of the understanding is our essentially optimistic belief in the feasibility of developing intellectual pursuits and research activities that can illuminate the critical issues of the age and aid in shaping sane choices. Self-interest is at the center here, clearly; the survival of the university and of society are primary goals.

But we are also aware of the importance of the role of educational settings in bringing together widely divergent noncommunicating sectors of society. "A democracy," said Dewey many years ago, "is more than a form of government. It is primarily a mode of associated living, of conjoint communicated experience." And in explaining his point, the philosopher enlarged on democracy as a psychological as well as political state—a condition of mutual sympathy—and held that the advance of democracy amounts in essence to "the extension in space of the number of individuals who participate in an interest so that each has to refer his own action to that of others, and to consider the action of others to give point and direction to his own. . . ." The real goal of "breaking down those barriers of class, race, and national territory which keep men from perceiving the full import of their activity" is precisely to achieve extended participation, for all people, in interests not immediately their own.(6)

It would be a mistake to cast the cause of change in graduate education wholly in a mold of do-goodism. Evaluating projects as contributions to the health of democracy can lead to atrophy of the imagination; the much abused slogans—learning for learning's sake, art for art's sake—contain an edge of truth, namely that the desire to do good is far from the most powerful spring to creativity.

But we do not believe that creativity will be harmed if graduate schools, in a manner appropriate to their distinctive character and function, become more conscious of their potential contribution in fostering "conjoint communicated experience," and aim more directly at familiarizing themselves with differences between accepted wisdom and current offcampus beliefs. This Panel has come to accept a philosophy of change whose ultimate conviction is that the values of disciplined curiosity and sympathetic responsiveness to that which differs from oneself can improve the moral and political health of the country, and advance knowledge as well.

The Panel does *not* believe that the university or the graduate disciplines can ever become sole custodian of all these values. But we are convinced of the link between the political spirit of liberty and the spirit of a genuinely humane and responsible intellectual enterprise. In thinking about this link we have not been hostile to the vision of freedom which stresses the right to self-exploration, self-involvement, containment in personal preoccupation or specialism. We have, however, ranked that vision a shade below Learned Hand's great formulation, which holds "the spirit of liberty [to be] the spirit which seeks to understand the minds of other men and women."(7)

Summary

A sound approach to change in graduate education will reflect a number of attitudes and assumptions, among them the following: respect for cognitive rationality as the surest means of advancing human knowledge; interest both in traditional pedagogy and in newer sources of information about where and how learning goes best; concern with how to make knowledge a more effective resource for meeting social needs. The foundation of such an approach lies in awareness that the cause of advanced knowledge cannot finally be separated from that of human aspiration generally. And the understood goals of change might be stated thus: To extend throughout the whole of society a vital scientific humanism, curious, sympathetic, alert to human difference, aware of interdependencies of individual and society, man and nature, and committed to the principle of free, disciplined inquiry.

IV: RECOMMENDATIONS

The 26 recommendations in this chapter are grouped in problem areas; the latter overlap at points, and, as will be apparent, many recommendations have a bearing on several topic areas besides those to which they are assigned. For purposes of clarity, the following pattern of presentation has been adopted: first a brief statement of the nature of the problem under consideration, followed by specific recommendations aimed at coping with the problem, and, finally, a summary of the Panel's reflections on ways of implementing its recommendations. (Some of the working papers, several of which provide additional suggestions concerning implementation, are listed at the end of this report.)

■ ■ ■ ■ ■ ■

Topic I: Clarification of Mission among Graduate Institutions

The problem in brief: Institutions awarding graduate degrees in the United States differ widely in function, but the meaning and value of this diversity remain obscure both inside and outside the academy. The opinion persists that a single standard, namely the quality of doctoral and postdoctoral research, is appropriate for the evaluation of the 307 graduate degree-granting schools which are currently members of the Council of Graduate Schools in the United States. Institutional behavior itself not infrequently reflects this delusion. Graduate programs with an orientation to teaching and to fulfilling the needs of regional or local student populations nevertheless can be pulled from their course by the influence of the major, national, comprehensive university programs. Equally harmful, diversity within the comprehensive universities themselves is inhibited by fear that evaluators will react negatively if they find deviations from the traditional norms of curricula, research, and the like. The possibility for cooperative relationships among any two graduate institutions performing different work is reduced because neither is likely to have a realistic understanding of the other's problems or proper goals.

The "problem of mission" only begins here. Its ramifications and implications extend beyond the uses of diversity. They touch not only the survival of graduate education but the future of several kinds of academic excellence as well. As we all know, steps are being taken now, at a variety of levels, to phase out graduate programs which, viewed from regional or other extra-institutional perspectives, appear redundant, and such actions have inhibited institutional powers of self-determination. But at the moment the severest threats lie in obliviousness to the need for earnest, objective self-scrutiny aimed at setting reasonable institutional goals in a regional context.

Specific Recommendations:

1. Graduate institutions and programs should undertake now to arrive at publicly articulated statements of their goals and functions. The statements should reflect: a) awareness of existing departmental strengths and weaknesses, and of the goals and functions of neighboring institutions of advanced education; b) the results of intensive faculty-administrative consideration of possible new directions for institutions that could assure them a significant identity related to their major resources.

2. Support should be sought for the creation of a commission to develop alternative standards of evaluation for graduate institutions not totally oriented to the standard of research eminence, and to apply these standards in assessing those institutions that want program evaluation.

3. The major comprehensive universities in a single geographic area, working with a state board of education or a regional agency, should attempt to clarify mission and function among graduate institutions in that particular area, and should, in addition, propose a blueprint for cooperative relationships among all the institutions in question.

On Implementation:

One can cite many recent examples of institutional self-examination that have resulted in shifts of focus and resource, and, at the same time, in clarifications of purpose. Success in such enterprises appears to depend heavily upon the capacity of leadership to be realistic and imaginative in considering their mission. The voice of realism is necessarily harsh. It asserts that graduate institutions are not exempt from the thrust of the new principle of accountability; graduate institutions that do not define special roles for themselves, demonstrate their commitment to those roles, and establish their particular capacity to fulfill them are likely to find one or another of their undertakings rated inessential by state coordinating boards, or other consultative agencies. If the institution does not arrive at a clarification of its own appropriate mission, in light of its resources and those of the competition, the clarification will be effected by outsiders.

Realistic tones of warning, though, need to be tempered by a sense of possibilities. For, while accountability is often perceived as a threat, it can also be regarded as a challenge. Those who ask institutions of advanced learning to justify themselves are, by that very deed, offering such institutions a chance to engage in self-study, and are, in addition, providing faculties and administrations alike with a way of achieving unified visions of purpose— visions with personal meaning for researchers, teachers, and students. To make the latter point, in conjunction with the former warning, requires a tactful balance of leadership. It means asserting simultaneously that graduate institutions failing to raise and answer questions of mission for themselves will find they have been assigned missions from outside, and that graduate faculties responding fully to this challenge may add to their power and dignity.

The precise composition of faculty-administration groups that can work with the technical panels referred to below (Topic IV, Recommendation 2) to clarify the question of mission should not be specified; each institution must find its own path. Nor is it useful to provide an inventory of possible institutional roles—the urban-oriented research center, the ecological institution, or the school of graduate study oriented toward regional training needs, to name a few. Handy catchall labels tend to obscure the need for a precise matching of roles and functions to institutional resources. Success in this undertaking requires faculty and administrative determination to seek out the true individuality of the institution, and a readiness to perceive that this search is at once a necessity and an opportunity.

One further word concerning Recommendation 3: Sensitive leaders of major graduate schools will be aware of the suspicion inevitably aroused by any effort on their part to "hand down" from above decisions about proper roles and functions for less well-established institutions in their areas. The task of introducing order and reason into graduate programs within a region is an exercise in negotiation, mutual explanation, and a recognition of aspiration; stern curbs on condescension are essential. It is unlikely that any proposal of a new role for a neighboring institution would be accepted unless it were accompanied by a particularized guarantee of long-term interinstitutional cooperation.

Topic II: The Problem of Access: Who Can't Go to Graduate School and Who Should

The problem in brief: Less than 3.5 percent of graduate enrollments in integrated institutions are Black students.(8) In 1970, less than 14 percent of the doctor's degrees awarded went to women,(9) and in 1967 only 9 percent of all United States full professors were women.(10) A hundred other statistics can be cited confirming that the politics of graduate education reflect the influence of a fundamentally sexist and discriminatory society. And the grip of this politics is currently being tightened by a funding crisis and shrinking job markets. Some efforts at reform are in progress, but the essential steps toward altering the basic patterns of access are still to be taken. The latter steps would radically change patterns of recruitment, employment practices, instruments of academic evaluation, and attitudes toward part-time study.

Specific Recommendations:

1. Efforts at recruiting able minority people and women to graduate faculties and student bodies should be intensified by every possible means.

2. The distribution of fellowship funds and other forms of financial aid, as well as attempts to secure new funds, should reflect the determination of graduate institutions to correct earlier biases in admission policy.

3. Assessments of capacity to pursue graduate work should be based on examination of all relevant information, including evidence concerning motivation and previous on-the-job achievements, and the practice of setting arbitrary cutoff points based on any index of ability should cease.

4. Course sequences, residence regulations, and other institutional requirements should be adapted to meet the needs of students with family responsibilities, adult learners, professionals, those forced to pursue their studies intermittently, and others whose admission to graduate education and preferred patterns of study differ from those regarded as standard.

5. Graduate departments should seek by all possible means to open up effective communication with extension divisions. There should be counseling about curricular offerings and full information provided about the meaning of extension credit, and the differences between extension and regular degrees.

On Implementation:

The major requisite action here can be bluntly stated: preferential treatment for those hitherto discriminated against. (Justification and precedents for this policy have recently been set forth in the Washington Supreme Court decision in the case of DeFunis v. Odegaard, and by Robert M. O'Neil in his 1971 *Yale Law Journal* survey of litigation concerning preferential admissions.(11)) It is one thing to advocate preferential treatment, however, and another to specify what must be done to insure that this policy brings about desirable outcomes. Recruitment and admission of victims of discrimination will by themselves accomplish little. Attitudinal change is equally important.

Graduate institutions must begin to break free from the stereotypes that have, until now, governed thinking about the part-time student. In the past, this student has been assigned inferior status, little or no financial aid has been available, and little effort or none has been expended in tailoring curricular patterns to his or her needs. If attempts to bring graduate study into closer demographic relationship with the population as a whole are to succeed in any but statistical terms, graduate administrators and faculties must arrive at a new perception of the worth and dignity of "recurrent" or "intermittent" learners, and of those whose entrance upon formal graduate study does not follow directly upon receipt of the baccalaureate.

It is also essential that graduate schools begin at once to prepare themselves for the tasks of developing new admissions criteria, new ways of evaluating motivation and job achievements, better methods of adapting styles of instruction to individual ways of learning, and firmer understandings of how to assess and further develop graduates of the newer contract-system and open admissions undergraduate institutions. Helpful material is already accumulating in several of these areas. Schools like the University Without Walls and Empire State College of the State University of New York have sufficient experience even now to counsel graduate institutions concerning the nature of the new materials and patterns of study with which they will shortly need to be conversant. The work on cognitive styles of learners has suggested ways in which graduate institutions can move beyond arbitrary guidelines in admissions policy—fixed cutoff points based on GRE scores, for one example—toward humane and intelligent analysis of performance prospects of students who do not qualify as gifted.(12) No amount of preparation for new student groups and styles, no amount of attitudinal correction, can be consequential unless accompanied by major changes in admissions policy: The *sine qua non* of progress on the problem of access remains preferential treatment; but it must be accompanied by a range of new behaviors and practices if its results are to be genuinely supportive, either of democratic aspiration or of effective advanced education.

Topic III: Nonacademic Experience as a Resource for Learning and Teaching

The problem in brief: Knowledge of how to evaluate competencies developed in nonacademic settings, and how to place these competencies usefully within academic settings, is essential to the contemporary graduate school; yet, practically speaking, such knowledge does not exist. The result is waste of a dozen serious kinds. Workers who face in mid-career the necessity of occupational recycling are often presented with graduate programs whose shape is unrelated to their abilities or their situation. The same problem confronts those who need refresher or updating courses. Furthermore, patterns of faculty recruitment remain unimaginative. Successful achievers in business and government possess gifts and experience that could be of immense influence in redirecting academic energies toward the servicing of social needs. This is equally true of community-based leaders and organizers. But both groups are seldom perceived as candidates for faculty positions; unverified by conventional academic qualifications, their experience and achievement appear impossible to assess. The prevailing assumptions about curricula and student and faculty evaluation come together in many areas to form a closed system, heedless of the variety of ways in which significant learning takes place in contemporary society.

Specific Recommendations:

1. Graduate departments should develop nondegree learning sequences to supplement regular degree programs, and should propose admissions mechanisms that would permit mature professionals to reenter graduate education, in a second or new vocational area, on a special basis.

2. Graduate departments should develop ongoing, technical consultative panels composed of successful, nonuniversity-based doers in fields allied to the disciplines; these panels should meet regularly with the instructional staff for the purpose of providing suggestions concerning curricula, evaluative criteria—all matters related to advanced training.

3. Experts possessing career achievements in problem-solving should be appointed to graduate faculties, whether or not they can present the usual academic qualifications.

4. Support should be sought for an interinstitutional commission to develop techniques for establishing advanced placement and other equivalencies, at the graduate level, for work experience, and to serve as a permanent evaluative agency for such experience.

On Implementation:

The aim here is simultaneously to foster on-campus, lifelong learning and to insure that expertise developed in off-campus learning has appropriate influence in graduate education. Among the obstacles to be overcome are the following: inadequate communication between graduate schools and industry, government, and community about the kinds of career and mid-career training currently most needed; uncertainty about how to evaluate work achievements in intellectual/academic terms; the difficulty of insuring, under a tenure system, the prestige of outstanding achievers in problem areas who might neither seek nor desire academic tenure.

The Panel believes that better guidance in constructing non-degree learning experiences and clearer measures of equivalencies between advanced academic study and high-level managerial and other achievement can be met, in significant part, through joint labor by faculty members and the consultative technical panels called for in Recommendation 2. The functions of the panels we have in mind would be more precisely stated than is typically the case with ordinary visiting committees; the membership would include leaders possessing relevant occupational expertise on which to base suggestions for curricular innovation. Further help with problems of evaluation should be sought from studies of techniques refined in the civil service and the military for rating performance and responsibility.

As for guaranteeing the prestige of nontenured professionals and community leaders, it appears probable that an entirely new mode of adjunct professional appointment will be necessary, with adjustments of salary and other items to insure parities of influence.

No single set of proposals in these areas is universally practicable; procedures will and should vary in accordance with institutions and disciplines. Nor does the Panel wish to minimize the intricacies of the task. Some successes in defining equivalencies have been registered in the past— predictably, at the lower and at the highest rungs of intellectual achievement. It is now accepted that high school diplomas can reasonably be awarded for particular kinds of work achievement; and the record shows that independent scholars lacking the doctorate who demonstrate, through publication of definitive research results, or through patents, their preeminence in a field have been invited to join graduate faculties. In the middle range of experiential achievement, however, what constitutes academic credit is obviously harder to determine.

Yet there has been very little research on this subject. The Panel believes that, in the interests of protecting the graduate institution, or at least some of its parts, from the dangers of parochialism and isolation from society, the question must now be taken up in earnest.

Topic IV: Alienation in the Student-Faculty Community

The problem in brief: Particularly for graduate students with slight adult experience of nonacademic life and no opportunity for participation in team research in a lab or elsewhere, the period of graduate study often resembles a chamber of alienation: Access to contemporaries, older colleagues, and to fellow citizens in the community outside the academy is sharply limited. One harmful effect is the intensification of a sense of removal from societal concerns. Another is a failure to develop participational skills—a highly consequential failure in men and women of trained intellect. Still another is perception of graduate study, by the student, as an act of retreat or postponement rather than of present engagement; the student lacks clarity about the importance of his activity here and now not only for himself but for his seniors, his institution, and his culture as a whole.

Specific Recommendations:

1. In every discipline, and especially at the Ph.D. level, graduate training should include, for all candidates who do not already possess such experience, a deliberate and significant component of discipline-related work outside the university walls.

2. In every discipline, joint, elected, student-faculty committees should be created for the purpose of maintaining a dialogue on matters of common interest, including requirements for the degree and decisions about departmental research emphases and budget priorities.

3. Administrative authorities and faculty members in a position to do so should seek by every available means to strengthen a view of advanced study as a cooperative, learning-research, problem-solving venture in which students and faculty contribute interdependently as adults engaged in pursuits essential to the future of human society.

On Implementation:

Stated generally, the aim here is to increase access to social reality. A discipline-related work experience can be a way of acquainting the graduate students with perspectives on his knowledge and values that prevail in the general society. That experience should also serve to alert the student to problems of community life on which his knowledge has bearing, and help him to achieve a more proportioned understanding of nonacademic opinion. The terms and sites of placement would vary widely, but stereotyping (such as all predoctoral scientists placed in industry, all predoctoral humanists placed in classrooms) should be resisted. Students in the arts and humanities might hold apprentice places on media staffs, in marketing or advertising concerns, in cultural centers, ecological agencies, in galleries, museums, and theaters. Decisions concerning the general nature of each graduate student's off-campus work would be made by the student in consultation with a graduate advisor at the inception of advanced study. Problems of placement would be met by departmental officers drawing ultimately on the aid of consulting groups composed of managers of offcampus enterprises in business, industry, government, and the community that are linked to the discipline. (See Topic III, Recommendation 2.) The student's report or journal of his work experience, in particular his account of its bearing on his studies and on his preference in terms of specialty, would become part of his official graduate record; so too would evaluative materials concerning his or her performance supplied by colleagues at the work site.

The burdens and difficulties entailed in this recommendation are considerable, and the Panel members have weighed them at length. Study-related work opportunities exist and can at length be mastered, as the performance of several undergraduate institutions attests, but the initial barriers are intimidating, and a measure of frustration can be anticipated.

Students in large universities in rural settings might have no choice except to relocate, for three to six months, to areas where work connected with the field would be readily obtainable; married students would suffer the inconvenience of domestic dislocation. And there will surely be a continuing protest that field experience is irrelevant to this or that branch of study. It is not as yet a received truth that a doctoral candidate whose special field is, for instance, the monarchy in seventeenth-century France would be markedly improved as a scholar or teacher if he worked on a contemporary local or business history project. The uses of field work in many areas will have to be demonstrated; they cannot simply be assumed.

Imposing as the obstacles are, however, they seem less troubling than the consequences of further prolonging insular modes of graduate study. In order to implement this recommendation without placing burdens on themselves that cannot be carried, departments will need to move gradually, setting goals from year to year in light of realistic appraisals of offcampus placement opportunities, and avoiding the practice of laying down permanent uniform requirements. Graduate faculties cannot create or appraise offcampus placement by themselves; business, government, and the community have essential roles to play. But the initiatives must come from within the graduate institution; theirs is the prime responsibility for revealing the links between the world of work and advanced scholarship and the ways in which it is possible for men and women of every age to function as scholars for society.

The function of the student-faculty committees called for by Recommendation 2 is to insure continual reexamination of requirements in light of the evolution of a discipline and its changing relation to social need and to promote joint student-faculty decision making where appropriate. Areas in which such decision making, subject to review, appear desirable include residence requirements, foreign language requirements, general oral examinations, final oral examinations, procedures for gaining acceptance of topics for doctoral research, preparations for the writing of the thesis, and methods of building intellectual community and solidarity among younger faculty launching doctoral projects. The committees may also be useful as clearinghouses for student opinion concerning the teaching effectiveness of candidates for tenure appointment.

The assumption in Recommendation 3 is that graduate students and faculty alike often tend to overestimate the significance of the product of graduate study (the degree) and to underestimate the significance of the process. Administrators can work to correct this misevaluation in a variety of ways: by stressing existing opportunities (and creating new ones) for joint intellectual participation by students and faculty in problem solving related to the larger life of the society; by publicizing specific instances of collaboration between elders and juniors; by employing members of the technical panels (see Topic III, Recommendation 2) on faculty committees, including examination committees; by emphasizing graduate training as a preparation for a career rather than for the first job; and by representing the activities of research and study both within and beyond the walls as integral to the advance of civilization, rather than as a mere route to a degree.

Topic V: Inequities and Omissions in the Reward System

The problem in brief: Current yardsticks for measuring faculty performance are irrelevant to many important activities of graduate professors. Attempts by younger teachers to develop innovative cross-disciplinary projects in research or teaching may receive verbal encouragement from administrative authorities; tenured graduate faculty who devote a portion of their energy in an attempt to improve instruction and curriculum may earn regard from their colleagues as selfless citizens; students and faculty who work together in task forces, attempting to apply their knowledge to areas of community need, may receive the gratitude of civic leaders.

But scales for the evaluation of these efforts neither exist nor are sought after by academic leaders. One result is that men and women who conceivably could contribute important work in the areas mentioned are discouraged from even entering them. Another result is that many who venture into such areas successfully are repeatedly distracted by the need to "cover themselves professionally" through publication—often writing papers less significant to the cause of knowledge than the very project that is interrupted. Still another result is that younger idealistic professionals who commit themselves, on the invitation of their tenured seniors, to unconventional projects for which no orthodox academic publication can be expected, pay for their cooperativeness (or impressionability) at the moment when tenure committees review their records. By announcing that only one kind of distinction is possible for academic man or woman, the publication system insinuates that any inclination to move in different directions is a certain badge of the second-rate. The overall effect is to further widen the breach between advanced knowledge and society.

Specific Recommendations:

1. University deans and department chairmen, working with faculty members,
42   should make a detailed inventory of all faculty activities considered

worthy of pursuit. Following completion of the inventory, the same authorities should develop standards for the evaluation of the activities, each considered as an independent enterprise. Thereafter these academic leaders should see to it that assessments of faculty for tenure, promotion, and salary increments are no longer based on the single criterion of research and publication but reflect a scrupulous and critical survey of the quality of performance in these other legitimate forms of intellectual enterprise.

2. When a faculty member, in submitting evidence of accomplishment, cites participation in a community venture, salary and tenure reviewers should accept evaluation of the performance by the teacher's colleagues, both academic *and* nonacademic, in the undertaking in question.

3. The broader-ranging scales of assessment implied in Recommendations 1 and 2 above should be publicly circulated, so that every faculty member will know in advance what weight an oncampus or offcampus obligation carries when faculty distinction is assessed and the terms in which distinction is to be measured.

On Implementation:

Moving beyond pieties about the desirability of rewarding good teachers or the academic contributions of non-traditional character means, first, securing more orderly and reliable means of assessing teaching performance, and, second, expanding faculty and student awareness of the range of ways in which noteworthy intellectual contributions can be made. As matters stand in many institutions, information about the quality of a graduate faculty member's teaching is collected neither regularly nor systematically. What is more, issues of educational style and goals are rarely discussed in departments or disciplines. The Panel understands that certain accomplishments of distinguished undergraduate teachers—for example, awakening students to the excitement or beauty of a subject matter area approached for the first time—are less likely to occur at the graduate level. And certainly it serves the interest neither of teaching nor of scholarship to pretend that there are no differences between the two, or that a brilliantly shaped lecture introducing a field of inquiry and an original research achievement within the field are one and the same thing.

But in the opinion of this Panel it is both essential and possible for pedagogical issues to figure more openly in the world of graduate study. Individual faculty members should indicate, either in conferences or through questionnaires, their eagerness for information about the impact of their courses or projects as perceived by their students, not only at the close of a term but throughout its duration. Efforts to identify modes of excellence in graduate-level teaching and to single out distinguished performances by individuals should be continuous. Graduate faculty-student committees should foster informal discussion series on problems in teaching and should serve as sounding boards through which opinion about the quality of the day-to-day teaching performance can be expressed. Underground ratings, student grapevines, and the like are, admittedly, untrustworthy sources of information for tenure and promotion committees. The opinions they reflect are relatively unsophisticated, have not been examined from the point of view of the assumptions governing them, and do not flow from open speculative interchange among teachers and students. When adequate openness has been achieved in this area, it should become possible to arrive at standards that can serve as solid criteria for reward.

It needs restating, however, that, if the reward system is ever to be genuinely sound, it cannot limit itself to consideration of teaching quality only or original research contributions, or both. A graduate faculty member may demonstrate intellectual effectiveness in an extraordinary variety of ways: by creating and carrying to a successful conclusion significant research projects in learning and teaching for special instructional seminars in the humanities; by developing new software in a field of educational technology; by performing leadership functions within the committee structure, advancing proposals concerning curriculum and governance, or aiding in the resolution of faculty-administrative tensions; by inventing new ways in which to locate the expertise of outside professionals within the teaching arrangements of the graduate school; by inventing new ways in which to use academic knowledge outside the university in effective community service; by developing innovative teaching and learning strategies; by imaginatively assessing credit from work experience for placement, both for the experiential component of graduate education and professional employment.

Of course, the degree of weight to be attached to any performance will vary with the function and mission of a department or institution. The Panel believes it would be harmful to the cause of diversity if uniform standards for distinguishing among faculty performances were to be adopted by all graduate institutions. The point is that fairness in a reward system demands open acknowledgement of the many kinds of activity that the individual graduate institution regards as proper and valuable to a school engaged in its particular kinds of undertaking, and, finally, recognition that measurable differences in quality of performance can be discerned in a variety of undertakings besides traditional teaching and research.

Topic VI: The Use of New and Neglected Media

The problem in brief: As a result of a continuing and often badly confused debate about its merits, the new educational technology has yet to be generally recognized for what it is: a pivotal resource for the democratization of learning. Those who argue that this technology increases passivity among students, or that it mechanizes or depersonalizes the learning process, are often well-intentioned and sincere. And the same can be said for those who fear the new media because of a conviction that media producers, trained in the arenas of entertainment, will never be capable of understanding or respecting the structural integrity of an intellectual discipline. But this resistance is misconceived and the delays it has caused in the refinement and use of existing technology approach the scandalous.

Scholars prepared to see themselves as philosophical guides to their discipline, rather than as platform lecturers, could draw on libraries of taped and filmed lectures in their fields, and bend their own energies more directly to the work of individualized counseling with advanced students. Leaders in special fields within the disciplines who cooperate with media experts to create introductions to their disciplines that are suitable for use in non-research oriented institutions could contribute greatly to the understanding of their advanced intellectual enterprise. Specialists who work for a period with computer technologists and education researchers on projects aimed at opening up the codes of high culture and advanced learning would surely improve the prospects for democratization.

And, possibly more important than any of this, full exploitation of the technological promise could lead to the abolition of educational lockstep, in time and space, and bring on a whole new teaching era for the elite as well as the disadvantaged—a time in which vividly individualized instruction, geared to personal idiosyncrasy and learning patterns, would become the norm. But the richness of the possibilities in these areas continues to go largely un-noticed. Even among those who count themselves enthusiasts of technological innovation, costcutting is virtually the only aspect of the subject that presently commands intense interest.

Specific Recommendations:

1. Graduate institutions should encourage research and innovation in the field of education. There is particular need for research in the teaching/learning process and the proper use of emerging technological aids for instruction.

2. Wherever high-quality, new media make it feasible, department chairmen should seek reductions in graduate-level lecture courses and increases in graduate seminars and research colloquia.

3. Every graduate institution, regardless of its chosen mission, should explore new instructional materials and conduct faculty and student workshops in the uses and possibilities of the emerging technologies.

45

On Implementation:

The surest way to stimulate faculty interest and action in exploiting existing educational technology is through demonstrations of its present capabilities. A striking showcase of those capabilities is the University of Illinois' PLATO IV project.(13) The reason for this is twofold: With the aid of certain new inventions permitting the student at a console to send as well as receive messages in a variety of ways, PLATO permits levels of interaction between learner and preceptor higher in some respects than those common in conventional classrooms. And, in addition, the PLATO system (through the use of an ingenious new invented language) makes it possible for teachers with orthodox training and no experience as computer programmers to learn how to write, modify, and edit lesson materials in their fields at any student station. Spokesmen for the Computer-based Education Research Laboratory at Urbana have noted that more than 500 authors from at least 40 disciplines or professional fields and from more than 20 institutions are now actively engaged in the development of instructional materials. Many of them are carrying out research to evaluate the effectiveness of this medium.

Many uses for such technology at the graduate level come to mind—for instance, it could be a means of introducing a new discipline to a researcher desiring to explore, rapidly and economically, a branch of knowledge that may have bearings on his own research. But what matters more than particular immediate uses of this technology is the radical demonstration of its capabilities. It is necessary to repeat that the implementation of the recommendations above depends upon sharp awareness of the educational breakthroughs implicit in the new technology. Firsthand acquaintance with the PLATO project tends to intensify that awareness.

Topic VII: Toward a New Conception of Subject Matter

The problem in brief: A number of disciplines are currently bound by convention, traditional forms, and revered research preoccupations. It is true that no discipline can advance without developing special problem areas for research. But insufficient attention is sometimes paid to the price of that process. The movement toward ever higher standards of professionalization has begun to obscure the meaning and uses of many areas of humanistic knowledge. And the tendency to dismiss as "unreal" areas originally excluded only because they appeared inconvenient for inquiry is evident throughout advanced study. Every discipline is a culture; every culture is a mode of repression; the current problem in several disciplines is that the nature and grounds of the relevant repressions have been forgotten or else sanctified (less by reason than by superstition). The losses of authority and range of reference to the public world are severe.

Specific Recommendations:

1. Especially in research-oriented institutions, discipline-based seminars on essential subject matter should be created every three to five years. The function of these seminars should be to examine prevailing methodologies of teaching, to probe neglected areas of social reference and the border points of the discipline as they are presently understood. In addition to graduate faculty and students, participants in the seminar should include experts from outside the university, prospective employers of degree candidates within the program of study, and selected members of the technical panels for the discipline (see Topic III, Recommendation 2).

2. Professional associations, particularly in the humanities, should periodically appoint blueribbon committees of inquiry charged with the task of scrutinizing current academic understandings of the social uses and provenance of the major disciplines. These committees should be composed of outstanding scholars and of professionals functioning inside *and* outside the academy.

On Implementation:

A Panel composed of a membership as varied as ours cannot speak in a single voice about possible new conceptions of subject matter or say what the neglected areas of social reference in any particular discipline might be. The task demands concentrated labor, discipline by discipline, by those who are involved in each special field of knowledge. When this is said, however, it needs to be added that, in more than a few disciplines, scholars of the highest rank have lately declared their belief that questions regarding the nature of the fundamentals of the discipline are becoming urgent. Writing in a recent issue of *Daedalus*, the noted scholar and critic Northrop Frye traced the development, over the past few decades, of patterns of study and research in English, moving from traditions of philological and historical research to the protest against both in the so-called new criticism, and remarking that the latter school "lost itself in a labyrinth of explanation." Frye's contention was that English over the decades had adopted a kind of false scientization that narrowed the range of meaning and reference of literature as a whole. He concluded: "I think that enough theoretical work has been done now to make visible a shift of emphasis, and that we are at the beginning of another phase of scholarship . . . There may again be some specialization and division of labor, but the old pseudo-scientific analogy has had it."(14)

Implicit in the writer's words is a sense that the moment is near for a fresh formulation of the aims and directions of this particular area of advanced study and research. And, as we have noted, scholars in a number of fields in the social and natural sciences are currently speaking in a similar vein. The terms of the new formulations cannot now be predicted. Moreover, it is not the intention of the present Panel, in singling out the field of literature, to assert that the need for stocktaking, and for awareness of fundamental change in understanding the very nature of the subject, is more urgent in this field than, say, in the field of physics. Probably in every subject matter, periodic return to basic questions is essential—questions concerning fundamental assumptions about life-reference, and concerning the possibility that a cycle of research activity has brought new, underpublicized, hence unrecognized conceptions of the subject into being. We believe that initiatives in this direction should originate in the profession at large, acting through major, discipline-oriented institutions.

Topic VIII: Insuring Viable Futures

The problem in brief: The current beleaguerment and crisis in graduate education stems in part from failures of awareness within the institutions themselves—insufficient alertness to trends in societal needs, employment opportunities, student interests, and external funding opportunities. But while steps can be, and are now being, taken to meet the current problems, there is a clear need for built-in, enduring mechanisms to prevent graduate institutions from again sliding out of touch with social reality. The problem in one of its dimensions can be stated as a question: How can advanced educational communities be stimulated into long-range planning that simultaneously enhances diversity and commitment?

But here again there are broader dimensions. Certainly the present time is a period of transformation for all institutions; churches, political parties, agencies of government, and organs of communication have lately been confronting fundamental problems of role and identity. The university effort at redefining its relationship to public concerns has many points of connection with comparable efforts by the larger corporations. The anxiety besetting faculties as they seek a new perspective on the function of universities has a direct counterpart in corporate board rooms.

This very similarity of situation—and the quality of anxiety—is a clue to the nature of the deeper problem at hand. That the corporation and graduate school are often almost equally harried in their attempts to stay abreast of change, to adapt to new currents of taste and aspiration, signifies not merely the absence of mechanisms for effective long-range planning. It signifies that another responsibility of highly trained intelligence—that of providing intellectual leadership in mapping the future by clarifying the choices society must soon make—has not been seized. In the largest terms, the problem of a viable future is more than insuring that the pursuit of new knowledge can be continued in graduate school settings. It is a matter of recreating the graduate faculty as *leaders* in the search for a new understanding of the possibilities of human society and of recreating the graduate institution as one that is capable of counseling political and cultural leaders on ways of assuring meaning to the structural changes of society now in progress.

The necessary steps cannot be taken unless the graduate faculties become more skillful in accommodating themselves to social change. But such adeptness will not be enough. The essential problem is the survival not only of graduate institutions but of a whole society in transformation. Managing these transformations, looking ahead, concentrating attentively enough on the structural complexities and interdependencies of social and technological change—this, clearly, is a task for advanced intelligence. Yet at this moment few graduate institutions have begun to approach these problems.

Specific Recommendations:

1. Administrators and faculty at each institution should undertake now to create and fund permanent long-range planning groups to develop, through research, consultation, and other broad-based inquiry means of insuring successful institutional adaptation to environmental change.

2. With the aid of the planning groups, departmental chairmen should prepare periodic reports on all discipline-related information vital to effective long-range planning.

3. By interinstitutional discussion among the above planning groups about social and technological choices, and through interdisciplinary task forces engaged in future-oriented policy studies, universities should press for the development of ways in which advanced intelligence within graduate institutions can contribute to the design of viable communities for the future.

On Implementation:

The primary requisite for implementation here is attitudinal change. If graduate institutions remain preoccupied with merely amending their own past inflexibilities, the likelihood is small that the pivotal role we envisage for the graduate school in societal planning can be taken up. But the step forward to a new understanding of function cannot take place without leadership. It is essential that leaders in graduate education become advocates of "future orientation." Leadership must make clear that, to be effective, highly trained intelligence needs to acknowledge and to develop its own power of anticipation, its ability to trace out patterns and options obscured in the managerial centers of a technological society by day-to-day urgencies. Again, no single contrivance can guarantee a concern with tomorrow; we are speaking of what amounts, at bottom, to a way of perceiving ultimate uses of intelligence. The roots of this perception lie in openness to the worth and purposefulness of intellectual labor aimed at inventing a habitable future.

49

V: PROJECTIONS

At the time it accepted the assignment to survey approaches to graduate study, this Panel was not offered and probably would not have accepted an approved blueprint for the future, utopian or otherwise. The lines of our inquiry were shaped partly by our panelists' firsthand knowledge of trouble spots in the existing system and partly by the growth of consensus among us concerning the role of advanced study and research at this stage in the development of democratic society. Our way of working was first to define problems and thereafter to consider possible solutions that we presented in the form of our recommendations.

The absence of a blueprint at the start, however, does not mean that we considered the relations among the changes proposed to be obscure or that we operated without a sense of the interdependency of the major issues. Structural and procedural changes of a high order of magnitude, like those proposed in the recommendations, are likely to work together. And precisely because of this, we must also understand that such changes have a cumulative impact.

The Future Graduate Students

The composition and activities of the future student body will differ significantly from those typical today, but there will be many continuities. The student population will be fairly evenly divided between the sexes; at least 20 percent of its number will be drawn from minority groups; because of career recycling and new patterns of recurrent education, the ages of students will correspond more closely to those of the general population. Settings for graduate work will be various, and there will be a sense of the campus as one resource center among many. A doctoral candidate in political science might have a job in a store-front civic literacy center in a low income housing project; a doctoral candidate in social psychology might work in a neighborhood educational counseling center; a doctoral candidate in comparative literature might teach in a remedial reading clinic; candidates in biology and chemistry might team up to study and correct deterioration in the local environment.

Traditional methods of evaluating student performance will be supplemented, and in some instances replaced, by continuous processes of critical interaction among teachers, students, and others as members of teams working toward shared goals, and by new modes of communication between learners and teachers flowing from technological advances. It will be standard practice for students and teachers alike to examine the social implications of projected research. Students whose community experience leads them to perceive a need for social change will participate in attempts to secure the necessary change, recognizing the pertinence of such efforts to the education of competent professionals. Wherever possible, course work and independent research will be joined organically with student-faculty problem-solving efforts. Stages in a person's career as graduate student— completion of residencies, scheduling of examinations, termination points of individual research—will be determined in part by the rhythms of progress in the team effort engaging him; catalog-specified requirements will serve as guidelines, but not as law.

Future Faculty Activity

Standards for measuring faculty performance will be applied to a great variety of professional activities. Explicit commitments concerning credit toward tenure and promotion to be assigned different types of faculty tasks (special committee work, the development of new undergraduate courses, and the like) will be made administratively before these obligations are accepted. Political and other community activity will be assessed, if the faculty member wishes, as part of his record of accomplishments. Because of expanded use of new educational technology, the graduate professor's role will increasingly be that of mentor and preprofessional counselor. The dynamics of faculty interaction with students will develop both through the mentor relationship, and through student-faculty collaboration in committees on departmental matters of common concern. A portion of many faculty members' time will be devoted to cooperative ventures aimed at improving and teaching of their subjects in institutions performing different functions from that of their own. Faculty circles, social and intellectual, will be more diversified for a number of reasons, among them the new male-female ratios and minority representations, the presence of nonacademic professionals serving in numbers on problem teams, with faculty status, the establishment of offcampus centers of learning and teaching, and the development of departmental business-government consulting groups.

Future Community Relations

The distance between the university and society will be narrowed, owing to
52   the de-emphasis of degrees, the shaping of flexible patterns of recurrent

study, the acceptance of a range of work and life experience for academic credit, the use of technology in individualized programs of instruction, both on and off campus, and increased concern at every academic level to the service of social needs. Significant lines of communication will connect graduate programs and schools of different functions with each other and with colleges of liberal arts, two-year colleges, state departments of education, and advanced training programs in industry and government. Collaborative enterprises involving curricular consultation will be common. Community colleges in process of developing new basic programs in any of the disciplines will be able to turn to their affiliated graduate institutions for advice and planning. New institutional forms will evolve independently at the university, for the purpose of fostering collaboration among government officials, political leaders, business executives, and academics. In time, other new institutional forms bringing faculty and society together directly—as, for example, Advanced Education Counseling and Action Centers—will come into being. As levels of understanding grow between university and society, a principle of cooperative accountability will win tacit approval from both.

Curricula and Careers

The order and procedure of advanced study in every discipline will be related not alone to the inner structure of the discipline but to other considerations as well. One consideration will be whether the student is enrolling for the purpose of self-development or to prepare for a particular professional career or career change; another consideration will be whether the function of the institution offering the courses is primarily the advancement of the discipline itself through research and experiment or that of training working professionals and paraprofessionals. Emphasis on whole problems will become a norm. Thus, ecological studies will combine work in the humanities, social sciences, natural sciences, and engineering, on the assumption that the attack on pollution requires attention not only to particles in exhausts but to drivers—their myths, instilled values, and aspirations.

Curricula will also reflect the view that cross-disciplinary studies are instruments for the creation of careers capable of meeting new social needs. Thus, interdisciplinary work in fine arts and urban studies will prepare curators whose management of urban cultural resources is in touch with community realities. Interdisciplinary work in the arts and in medical science will prepare instructors in both cultures to interact effectively in training programs that analyze physiological-psychological response. In general there will be an unremitting, although not intimidating challenge to the more restrictive, exclusionary features of disciplinary cultures; the challenge will be laid down partly on the ground that existing social problems cannot be met except through unprecedented combinations of bodies of knowledge, and partly because the genuine points of connection among the disciplines deserve exploration for their own intrinsic interest. The content of advanced education from discipline to discipline will, however, change less than the forms. The primary change will come from the emphasis on the public uses of knowledge. As one writer puts it, discussing innovation in medical education, "the skills and knowledge of the past will still apply; it is the assumptions and ideas of the past as to how that knowledge was to be put into human service that [will] change."(15)

Changes in Attitudes

The most effective leadership in initiating and responding to the changes described will come from those continuously alert to the ways in which each part works on every other part in the struggle to enlarge a vital intellectual culture in a democratic society. Sustaining this alertness means bearing simultaneously in mind achievements, dangers, and opportunities. The achievements are those of the graduate institution as they exist now. Leadership will need to remind itself of the function of graduate schools as models of intellectual culture, as embodiments of aspirations higher than that of mere comfort, and especially as agents of cultural memory—means, that is, of renewing from generation to generation appreciative knowledge of tastes and accomplishments and values that the fashion of any given contemporary period might have discarded.

If the terms "tradition," "preservation of values," and "cultural heritage" are worn, the deeds of mind and imagination to which they point are not. Ten thousand things difficult and beautiful in art and science—these continue to be passed along to the future because institutions of advanced knowledge have continued to commit themselves, despite numberless beleaguerments, to belief in their importance for man's moral and intellectual future. Powerful as the graduate institution's role has been in advancing knowledge, it does not outweigh the achievement of recovering and reevaluating the usable past. And it is inconceivable that the development of graduate institutions, as resources for human advance, can be furthered by men and women oblivious to that role.

Yet while all this is so, the changes proposed will almost certainly increase pressure on institutions to play the role of preserver less intensely than before. And effective leadership will need to be prepared for that turn of events, and should not pretend that danger is absent from the new equation. Closer relations between graduate school and community will bring new pressures to adjust to popular interest and may weaken allegiance to the truth that value resides in the demanding, the foreign, the ancient, and the strange, as well as in their opposites. Leadership will have to face squarely the facts that the present age sets few restraints on self-expression, personal ambition, and personal choice, and that the new freedom to aspire is often accompanied by resentment at the difficulty of translating aspiration into achievement. Invited to participate in higher learning, given the run of its house, those who chafe at discipline, or are humiliated by it, sometimes see themselves as having been morally (and wrongly) indicted. Men and women of good will, instructors who know the irrelevance of fault and blame in these areas but are frustrated in their effort to communicate this to others, have been known to turn against their own perception of worth, even to damn their own kind as elitists. The danger is that, as the distance narrows between ordinary life and the world of complex learning, the provocations and enticements to pointless self-laceration are bound to multiply.

A task for leadership is to establish the ground of resistance to these enticements. On the one hand, this entails explaining persuasively why it is wholly natural that many of the academy's best achievements are not respected by people who profess an appetite for what advanced learning can offer. On the other hand, it entails encouraging teachers and scholars to imagine the terms on which these appetites could be nourished and purposeful "conjoint communicated experience" could take place. What is essential, in other words, is a path between those who are affronted by the very notion of a closer relation between graduate learning and the society beyond the gates, and those whose responsiveness to admittedly urgent social needs drives them to fashionable deprecation of disinterested or "irrelevant" scholarship. Leadership will be obliged at one moment to insist that an anthropologist capable of brilliant readings of a Balinese cockfight as a significant cultural form, or a literary scholar capable of subtle study of relationships between versions of a myth found in a Rubens painting and in a Dryden translation would actually damage the prospect for a significant democratic culture if they were to abandon their inquiries in favor of some more immediate mode of community service.

Yet at the next moment leadership will find itself arguing that these scholars must not shut their eyes to current opportunities for extending awareness of the meaning and function of their kinds of activity through the general culture. The research scholar can and should at intervals interrupt himself for the purpose of adopting, imaginatively, the position that he can and should ask himself how his work, his goals, his procedures might be made more intelligible to nonscholars than they presently are. Further, this scholar can and should keep himself informed about the ways in which his discipline is represented in the worlds of learning beyond his peer group, and should contribute to the improvement of that representation. He should demonstrate to his students, by his own commitments, the necessity of pressing continually for more comprehensive and substantive communication with beginning learners in his field, regardless of their age or background. And the job of leadership is to create an atmosphere conducive to these behaviors.

That responsibility does not fall exclusively on the deans, chairmen, and senior faculty of the 700-800 institutions in the U.S. that now award graduate degrees. Initiative on the part of community and state college administrators, and indications of their readiness for significant relationships with schools of advanced learning, will help to close existing gaps. But the major burden will be borne by the graduate institutions themselves—a new obligation added to many already existing. The challenge, stated most simply, is to maintain a productive tension among the variety of obligations. Those who do so with greatest distinction will in all probability join intellectual power with enthusiasm for the prospect of diffusing that power through the culture as a whole, and with realism about the complexity of the task.

"The longer I live," said Péguy, "the less I believe in revolution—sudden, merciless, overnight—and the more I believe in modest, definitive, molecular social work."(16) As the members of this Panel have worked their way deeper into the structure of problems in advanced education, it has become clear to all that, while radical innovations are necessary and feasible, instant transformation of contemporary institutions is neither possible nor desirable. The redistribution of learning is not like the redistribution of purchasing power: It has no meaning except as it advances consciousness toward the love of knowledge for its own sake, as well as for its power. Yet if the processes by which men and women learn to relish these ideals are lined with ironies and paradoxes, even with seeming illiberalisms, they are nevertheless not as mysterious as privilege and complacency have often made them out to be. We believe the proposals for change offered here, if implemented, will help to open up these processes to fuller view. And we believe that, with the aid of patient, committed labor inside and outside the university walls, by all who understand the processes, the graduate community can move usefully closer to the society to which it belongs.

FOOTNOTES

1. John R. Valley, *Increasing the Options: Recent Developments in College and University Degree Programs.* Princeton, N.J.: College Entrance Examination Board and Educational Testing Service, 1972.

2. Various staff papers and research reports of the Commission on Non-Traditional Study were reviewed by the Panel, as was a prepublication copy of the final Commission report. Among these documents, the following were most useful to the study of graduate education:

Books

Commission on Non-Traditional Study, *Diversity by Design.* San Francisco: Jossey-Bass Publishers, 1973.

Cyril O. Houle, *The External Degree.* San Francisco: Jossey-Bass Publishers, 1973.

Samuel B. Gould, and K. Patricia Cross, eds., *Explorations in Non-Traditional Study.* San Francisco: Jossey-Bass Publishers, 1972.

Research Monographs

Abraham Carp, Richard E. Peterson, and Pamela Roelfs, *Learning Interests and Experiences of Adult Americans.* Princeton, N.J.: Educational Testing Service. (In preparation.)

Janet Ruyle, JB L. Hefferlin, L. A. Geiselman, and A. Kirton, *Non-Traditional Educational Opportunities and Programs in Traditional Colleges and Universities, 1972.* Princeton, N.J.: Educational Testing Service. (In preparation.)

Wesley W. Walton, *New Paths for Adult Learning: Systems for Delivery of Instruction in Non-Traditional Programs of Study.* Princeton, N.J.: Educational Testing Service. (In preparation.)

(These three monographs will constitute part of a book, *Planning for Non-Traditional Programs: An Analysis of the Issues,* by K. Patricia Cross, John R. Valley, and others, to be published by Jossey-Bass early in 1974.)

3. Carp, *et al. op cit.*

4. Harvey Brooks, "Thoughts on Graduate Education." *The Graduate Journal,* VIII: 2, 1971, p. 319.

5. Kenneth D. Roose and Charles J. Anderson, *A Rating of Graduate Programs.* Washington, D.C.: American Council on Education, 1970.

Allan M. Cartter, *An Assessment of Quality in Graduate Education: A Comparative Study of Graduate Departments in 29 Academic Disciplines.* Washington, D.C.: American Council on Education, 1966.

These publications represent only the most recent and widely known peer ratings. Several ratings limited to particular disciplines or schools have been published or circulated privately from time to time. So far as the Panel is aware, all such ratings follow the collegial reputation pattern of assessment set by Raymond Mollyneux Hughes in *A Study of the Graduate Schools of America*, published in Oxford, Ohio by Miami University in 1925.

6. John Dewey, *Democracy and Education*. New York: The Macmillan Company, 1916, p. 101.

7. Learned Hand, from "The Spirit of Liberty," a speech given at the I Am an American Day ceremony, New York City, May 21, 1944. Printed in Learned Hand, *The Spirit of Liberty: Papers and Addresses of Learned Hand*, collected, and with an introduction and notes, by Irving Dillard, . 3rd. New York: Alfred A. Knopf, 1960, p. 190.

8. I. Bruce Hamilton, *Graduate School Programs for Minority/Disadvantaged Students*. Princeton, N.J.: Educational Testing Service, 1973.

9. National Center for Educational Statistics, *Projections of Educational Statistics to 1980-81, 1971 Edition*. Washington, D.C.: Government Printing Office, 1972.

10. R. Simon, *et al.* "The Woman Ph.D.: A Recent Profile." *Social Problems*, vol. 15, 1967.

11. Robert M. O'Neil, "Preferential Admissions: Equalizing the Access of Minority Groups to Higher Education," *Yale Law Journal*, 80:4, March 1971, pp. 699-767.

12. There have been a number of published reports on cognitive styles research, which has been a subject of study since the late 1940's. A recent summary of the major findings to date and the implications for student selection and placement are contained in Herman A. Witkin, "The Role of Cognitive Style in Academic Performance and in Teacher-Student Relations," *Research Bulletin 73-11*. Princeton, N.J.: Educational Testing Service, February 1973. This report is adapted from a paper given at the Invitational Conference on Cognitive Styles and Creativity in Higher Education, Montreal, Canada, November 8-10, 1972.

13. D. Alpert, and D. L. Bitzer, "Advances in Computer-based Education." *Science*, vol. 167, March 20, 1970, pp. 1582-1590; and D. Alpert, "Communications Networks and Human Networks: PLATO IV, A New Computer-based Education and Communication System." A summary of

remarks presented at a workshop, "New Initiatives to Utilize Human Resources," held at Batelle Institute's Seattle Research Center, November 13-16, 1972.

14. Northrop Frye, "The Search for Acceptable Words." *Daedalus*, 102:2, Spring 1973, p. 13.

15. H. Jack Geiger, "The New Doctor," in Ronald Gross and Paul Osterman, eds., *The New Professionals*. New York: Simon and Schuster, 1972, p. 113.

16. Charles Pierre Péguy, *Pensées*. Paris: Gallimard, 1943, p. 75.

WORKING PAPERS OF THE PANEL

During the Panel's active life, a number of staff and committee papers were prepared to assist the Panel in its discussions. Several of those papers and reports listed below are available until supplies are exhausted. Copies may be obtained by writing to the Executive Secretary, Panel on Alternate Approaches to Graduate Education, Box 2607, Princeton, New Jersey 08540.

Committee on Populations Report. (Robert F. Kruh, Chairman) Committee paper analyzing the populations of potential students who are not well served by graduate education because of both traditional and conceptual deterrents to access. (undated, 15 pages)

Robert A. Feldmesser. "Problems and Issues in the Future of Graduate Education." Prepared for the Graduate Record Examinations Board meeting, March 11-12, 1971. (28 pages)

I. Bruce Hamilton. "Innovations in Graduate Programs: A Preliminary Report, November 1972." A summary of the responses to a letter sent by the Panel Chairman, Dr. J. Boyd Page, to the deans of institutions which are members of the Council of Graduate Schools. (with tables, 27 pages)

I. Bruce Hamilton. "Some Issues and Examples of Alternate Modes of Graduate Education: A Discussion Paper Prepared for the Panel on Alternate Approaches to Graduate Education, February 1972." (51 pages)

I. Bruce Hamilton. "Statistics on Graduate Education." A compilation of relevant figures drawn from the *Graduate Programs and Admissions Manual* and from reports issued by the National Center for Educational Statistics and the National Educational Association Research Division. (undated, 21 pages)

Elsa Rosenthal. "Some Current Issues in Graduate Education: A Review of the Literature 1965-1970." Prepared for the Graduate Record Examinations Board meeting, March 11-12, 1971. (18 pages)

BIBLIOGRAPHIC NOTE

A large number of reports, catalogs from non-traditional institutions, and publications were circulated to and by Panel members during the 18 months of the deliberations. Since these represent only a part of the store of knowledge brought by individuals to Panel meetings, and are not in any formal sense the basis for *Scholarship for Society*, they are not listed. Readers are urged to contact the Executive Secretary for information about materials pertaining to particular subjects.

The Panel would like to express appreciation to the Commission on Non-Traditional Study for its compilations of materials on programs initiated in recent years, particularly John Valley's *An Inventory of External Degree Programs and Proposals*, Princeton, New Jersey: Educational Testing Service, March 3, 1971, and a *Supplement to An Inventory of External Degree Programs and Proposals*, Princeton, New Jersey: Educational Testing Service, May 7, 1971.

Further thanks are due to the Office of Scientific Personnel of the National Research Council for its *Annotated Bibliography on Graduate Education, 1950-1971*, and the National Board on Graduate Education for its *Annotated Bibliography on Graduate Education, 1971-1972*. These bibliographies provided the most complete listings of recent materials available and were of considerable help to the Panel.

Scholarship for Society ORDER FORMS

ORDER FORM

I wish to order
_____ copies
of *Scholarship for Society* at
$_____
per copy.

☐ Enclosed is check
or money order
for $_____
payable to the
GRE Board.

☐ Please bill me.
(My order is for
10 or more copies.)

PANEL REPORT
GRE Board
Educational Testing Service
Princeton, NJ 08540

RETURN REQUESTED

540-90

no. copies

SPECIAL 4TH CLASS RATE—BOOKS

TO: _____

_____

_____

_____ ZIP CODE

ORDER FORM

I wish to order
_____ copies
of *Scholarship for Society* at
$_____
per copy.

☐ Enclosed is check
or money order
for $_____
payable to the
GRE Board.

☐ Please bill me.
(My order is for
10 or more copies.)

PANEL REPORT
GRE Board
Educational Testing Service
Princeton, NJ 08540

RETURN REQUESTED

540-90

no. copies

SPECIAL 4TH CLASS RATE—BOOKS

TO: _____

_____

_____

_____ ZIP CODE

ORDER FORM

I wish to order
_____ copies
of *Scholarship for Society* at
$_____
per copy.

☐ Enclosed is check
or money order
for $_____
payable to the
GRE Board.

☐ Please bill me.
(My order is for
10 or more copies.)

PANEL REPORT
GRE Board
Educational Testing Service
Princeton, NJ 08540

RETURN REQUESTED

540-90

no. copies

SPECIAL 4TH CLASS RATE—BOOKS

TO: _____

_____

_____

_____ ZIP CODE